THE AJE SPIRITS

The Secrets of Congo Initiations

PALO MAYOMBE - PALO MONTE - KIMBISA

CARLOS ANTONIO DE BOURBON-GALDIANO-MONTENEGRO

AMERICAN CANDOMBLE CHURCH PUBLICATIONS, LOS ANGELES, CALIFORNIA

THE AJE SPIRITS

The Secrets of Congo Initiations

PALO MAYOMBE - PALO MONTE - KIMBISA

AMERICAN CANDOMBLE CHURCH PUBLICATIONS

P.O. BOX 881377

LOS ANGELES, CALIFORNIA 90009

LEGAL DISCLAIMER

No part of this book may be reproduced in any manner without written permission from the publisher or the author of this book. This book contains formulas that were used in the historical AFRO-CARIBBEAN religious practices of Santeria, Palo Mayombe, Palo Monte and Kimbisa. The author and the publisher do not encourage any of the practices in this book nor do we assume any liabilities for presenting those formulas in this book. The formulas are presented for curious only. Neither the author nor the publisher, American Candomble Church assumes any responsibilities for the outcome of any of the spells, rituals or initiations in this book. We make no claims to any supernatural powers of these traditional initiation rituals. All inquiries or comments may be directed to the publisher. Warning: please be advised that all of the human bones and many of the animals used in these traditional magic formulas are available through biological supply distributors, taxidermy stores, zoos and museum stores. All of these items are available for sale on ebay. Grave digging, grave robbing and the use of endangered animals is illegal. Individuals must check with their individual state agencies and federal regulations to see if laws prohibit animal sacrifice, buying or selling of Human Bones and endangered animals. To investigate the legalities of animal sacrifice please refer to the Legal Case of "Hialeah vs. The Church of Lucumi" which established Santeria as a legitimate religion in the United States of America. You must be at least 18 years of age or older to purchase this book or to purchase any of the supplies listed herein.

TABLE OF CONTENTS

INTRODUCTION

The following book contains information about how to correctly prepare, make and present the sacred mysteries of the Aje Spirits initiation ceremony, Step by Step, (Regla De Congo).

This book also contains how to make a spiritual food offering to the witches (Adimu), various spells and sacred rituals to these very powerful elemental forces that we call "the sacred mothers of the marketplace" and the "invisible mothers of the night".

This book will tell you how to summon these powerful spiritual entities for such things as protection against the evil eye, love attraction, money, wealth, health, marriage, Divine Justice and a peaceful home.

The "*Aje Spirits Initiation Ceremony*" links our world to the invisible world of the *Aje Spirits* (Witches). The *Aje Spirits* control all aspects of human life such as wealth, health, prosperity, and our "*spiritual birth destiny*". If an individual does not undergo this initiation ceremony they will always be plagued with constant spiritual attacks by the *Aje Spirits*. By undergoing this initiation ceremony, an individual makes spiritual peace and establishes a lifelong relationship with the powerful *Aje Spirits* without any spiritual interference in order to be able to accomplish your desired goals in one's life.

The Three Fates (Aje Spirits).

THE AJE INITIATION CEREMONY

The *Aje Spirits* are invisible spiritual entities that coexist with humans here on Earth. It is believed that the *Aje Spirits* are powerful "*Witches*" that control all aspects of human destiny including such things as happiness, wealth, love, health and personal relationships. It is also believed that if an individual does not make a spiritual peace and truce with the powerful *Aje Spirits* that they can cause great harm and bring about great tragedy to all human beings. The *Aje Spirits* were here even before the first man and first woman appeared on this Earth. Since the time that man and woman first appeared here on Earth, the *Aje Spirits* have been in spiritual competition with humans and historically have many of times tried to eliminate all life of mankind through such negative acts as causing famines, disease and even natural catastrophes and disasters such as floods and earthquakes. By receiving the blessings of these powerful spiritual entities you will be establishing a personal relationship with them so they will not cause you any personal harm or misfortune. For all of these reasons just mentioned, that is why it is very important to receive their Mysteries before any other. If the *Aje Spirits* are not ritually appeased then an individual will never be able to fully accomplish their spiritual goals associated with their birth destiny. The *Aje Spirits Initiation Ceremony* takes 21 days to complete the ritual initiation ceremony. This ritual should be performed on a "*Full Moon*" at 12 midnight at the mountains, forest or in a field. The powerful *Aje Spirits* can be petitioned in all matters of spiritual protection, destruction, to wage war on your enemies, to kill your enemies in black magic death spells, to eliminate and to dominate your enemies and to cast various spells of attracting love, wealth and success to an individual. The *Aje Spirits* are identified with the "Fates" and the famous Greek statue of the "*Three Graces*" or in religious picture form as the "*Three Sisters,*" "*Faith, Hope & Charity*". There are several initiation formulas and ways to present the *Aje Spirits,* but the following is one of the most powerful and effective manners to do so. By following the initiation formula below you will see spectacular magical results.

If you are "not" currently initiated into the sacred mysteries of any *Trantional African Religious Tradition* you will still be able to prepare the sacred mysteries of the Aje Spirits which I will describe in detail within this book, but there are certain steps that you will not be able to do in the consecration ceremonial ritual. The mysteries of the Aje Spirits are very ancient and therefore no one man nor woman really has the authority over them to be able to say that they alone have the right to present these powerful mysteries. If you are involved with the mysteries of European withchraft from any tradition, you can prepare these very ancient sacred mysteries on your own. The only thing that you will not be able to do if you are not initiated into the mysteries of *Traditional African Religion* would be to make any blood sacrifice. Where there is a blood sacrifice listed in the steps of this book to prepare the Aje Spirits, you will have to substitute it with the strongest red wine that is available to you. Even though there are many individuals who would say that in order for this ceremony to be valid that it would require a blood sacrifice that is absolutely untrue because many of the sacred elements that go into the preparartion of the Aje Spirits already have spiritual energy found within it and are just waiting for some sort of divine activation and spiritual direction from you of how you would like to direct its energy to benefit you. An example of this would be the quartz crystals found within the actual Aje Spirits pot. Quartz crystals have their own spiritual energy which when used in combination with the sacred prayers to invoke the powerful Aje Spirit entities become activated and can be used in your favor during powerful sacred rituals and ceremonies. It must be remembered that the Aje Spirits have no real allegiance to any man or woman and therefore the relationship that develops between you and them will depend upon your actual spiritual intention and desires that exists between both of you. The relationship that will exist between you and the Aje Spirits will develop over a period of time. By preparing the mysteries of the Aje Spirits you are in reality celebrating their sacred mysteries out of respect for who they are and for what they represent to the Earth and to mankind. Because the Aje Spirits represent the four elements, which we (man) live in and need to survive, we therefore must give them respect and honor at all times if we want to live a peaceful and harmonius life with "Mother Nature" and "Mother Earth".

There are (5) sacred items that must be prepared in order to successfully give this initiation to an individual. Together all (5) sacred items are collectively called the "*AJE SPIRITS*". It is through these (5) very important religious items that the powerful *Aje Spirits* will be able to assist you when you summon them to our dimension from where they dwell. If you do not have all of the following sacred religious items at your shrine for the "*Aje Spirits*" they will not be able to manifest to you when summoning them. These (5) sacred religious items are the sacred "*OKOBELEFO*"(Clay Ceramic pot that will be housing the Mysteries of the Aje Spirits / Aje Spirits Nganga)", "*ORERE*" (Ozun De Aje)", "*TITILLERO*", (Hollow Gourd/Calabash), "*MPAKA*" and the "*MBELE*" (Machete).

The following initiation ceremony of how to present the Mysteries of the *Aje Spirits* is taken from the Afro-Caribbean Congo religious traditions of Palo Mayombe, Plao Monte and Kimbisa.

Although there are many initiation methods and variations of how to correctly present the *Aje Spirits,* if you follow this presented method you will witness and experience the spiritual power of the *Aje Spirits* in all of their "*Splendor and Glory*". If you have already received the *Aje Spirits Initiation Ceremony* and if their Mysteries were not presented to you in a manner similar to the following initiation ceremony then more than likely it was not done correct. If you have already been initiated as a member of a traditional Congo Munanzo and you have not received the *Aje Spirits* Mysteries you should seek out a qualified initiated individual who is familiar with the presentation and preparation of these very sacred and delicate mysteries to confer their "sacred mysteries" to you without delay. Once you have received the *Aje Spirits* Mysteries you will see your life start to change immediately over night into success. All of your everyday problems will completely vanish. The *Aje Spirits* can be used in the same magical and religious manner as you would use a traditional "*Congo Spirit Nganga.*"

* *ALL OF THE HUMAN BONES USED TO PREPARE THE AJE SPIRIT NGANGA MUST BE FROM FEMALE INDIVIDUALS* *

HOW TO PREPARE THE OKOBELEFO (AJE SPIRITS NGANGA)

ITEMS NECESSARY

1. *ONE LARGE CLAY CERAMIC POT WITH LID*
2. *TWENTY-ONE LIGHTNING STONES*
3. *NINE LARGE OBLONG STONES FROM THE TOP OF A MOUNTAIN*
4. *TWENTY-ONE QUARTZ CRYSTALS*
5. *ONE POUND OF MAGNETIC SAND*
6. *IRON OXIDATE POWDER*
7. *THREE SMALL METEORITE STONES*
8. *NINE PIECES OF SILVER*
9. *NINE PIECES OF GOLD*
10. *NINE PIECES OF COPPER*
11. *NINE PIECES OF BRONZE*
12. *NINE PIECES OF TIN*
13. NINE PIECES OF IRON
14. *THIRTY-SIX COINS FROM AROUND THE WORLD*
15. *DIRT FROM 121 TOMBS OF WOMEN*
16. *DIRT FROM THE MOUNTAINS/HILLS*
17. *DIRT FROM THE OCEAN'S EDGE*
18. *DIRT FROM THREE CHURCHES*
19. *SAND FROM THREE CROSSROADS*
20. *DIRT FROM A FIELD*
21. *DIRT FROM A FOREST*
22. *DIRT FROM THREE GATES*
23. *DIRT FROM THE INITIATES HOUSE (4 CORNERS OF THE PROPERTY)*
24. *NINE VENOMOUS SNAKES*
25. *NINE BATS*
26. *POWDERED BONES FROM 121 BIRDS OF FLIGHT*
27. *ONE GALLON OF OCEAN WATER*
28. *ONE GALLON OF RIVER WATER*
29. *ONE QUART MAY RAIN WATER* (OPTIONAL)
30. *POWDERED HUMAN BONES* (FEMALE)
31. *TWENTY-ONE PALOS IN POWDERED FORM*

32. *ONE POUND OF POWDERED DRIED LEAVES FROM A CEIBA TREE*
33. *ONE POUND OF POWDERED DRIED PALM LEAFS*
34. *ONE POUND OF POWDERED DRIED OAK LEAFS*
35. *21 FRESH HERBS* (SACRED TO THE SPIRIT OZAIN)
36. *DRIED SQUASH SEEDS*
37. *LIQUID MERCURY*
38. *VIRGIN CANDLE WAX*
39. *RED RELIGIOUS CANDLES IN GLASS* (7)
40. *RED PAINT*
41. *BLACK PAINT*
42. *CIGARS*
43. *RUM*

LIVE ANIMALS NEEDED

1. ONE BLACK ROOSTER
2. ONE BLACK HEN

PREPARATION

1. In a large mixing bowl, prepare an *Omiero* using the *(21) fresh herbs*. Use *(6) Grains of Paradise, River Water, Ocean Water, May Rain Water, Holy Water from a Church* and the *Milk* from *(6) Coconuts* in the preparation of the *Omiero*. After you have prepared the *Omiero (fresh herbs made into a liquid with fresh water)*, place the *Lightning Stones*, the *Meteorite Stones*, the *(9) Large Mountain Stones*, the *Quartz Crystals*, the *Coins*, the *Gold, Silver, Bronze, Tin, Iron, Copper Pieces* into the *Omiero* liquid and allow them to soak for a 24 hour period. Light the *Red Candles* and set next to the bowl of the *Omiero*. This procedure should be done outside.

2. Paint the *Spirit Signature* of the *AJE SPIRITS* with red and black paint on the inside bottom of the *Clay Bowl* and seal the design using melted *Virgin Candle Wax*.

3. After the *Wax* has dried, wash the inside and the outside of the *Clay Bowl* with some of the *Omiero* liquid.

4. Take a mouthful of *Rum* and spray it directly into the *Clay Bowl*.

5. Light a cigar and blow the smoke directly into the *Clay Bowl*.

6. After you have finished this procedure the vessel which will be housing the spirit has been ritually baptized and is now ready to receive the other items. Pour the mercury into the bottom of the large *Clay Bowl*.

7. In a large bucket, mix all of the *Dirts, Powdered Palos, Iron Oxidate Powder, Powdered Ceiba Leafs, Powdered Palm Leafs, Powdered Oak Leafs, Dried Squash Seeds* and the *Magnetic Sand* all together. Mix well.

8. After you have mixed all of the *Dirts* together, pour some of the *Omiero* liquid into the bucket along with the and make a thick past like mixture. The consistency being like a wet cement.

9. Using the past mixture, place a one inch layer over the design in the bowl.

10. On top of this mixture, place the *(9) Oblong Mountain Stones* into the center and the *21 Lightning Stones* positioned around the center of the *(9) Oblong Mountain Stones.*

11. Place the *Quartz Crystals* in a circle around the *lightning stones.*

12. After you have done this, place another layer of the thick dirt paste mixture on top of those items.

13. On this layer, place the *Gold, Silver, Copper, Bronze, Tin* and *Iron pieces.*

14. After you have done this, place another layer of the thick dirt paste mixture on top of those items.

15. On this layer, place all of the *Human Bone Powder.*

16. After you have done this, place another layer of the thick dirt paste mixture on top of those items.

17. On this layer place the *Bats.*

18. After you have done this, place another layer of the thick dirt paste mixture on top of those items.

19. On this layer place the *Powdered Bones of the Birds of Flight.*

20. After you have done this, place another layer of the thick dirt paste mixture on top of those items.

21. On this layer place the *(9) Venomous Snakes.* If they are still flexible, coil them up in striking positions.

22. After you have done this, place another layer of the thick dirt paste mixture on top of the other ingredients so that the dirt comes all the way up to the top of the clay pot.

23. Place the lid of the ceramic clay pot on top of it until you are ready to feed the *Aje Spirits*.

24. Proceed to the next step of preparing the "MPAKA", the "*ORERE*" (Ozun De Aje)", the "*TITILLERO*" (hollow gourd/calabash) and the "*MBELE*" (Ritual Machete).

HOW TO PREPARE THE MPAKA OF THE AJE SPIRITS

The "*Mpaka*" is perhaps one of the most important keys to the magical Spirit Mysteries of the Aje Spirit Nganga. The *Mpaka* Mysteries are always received and contained within the horn of an animal. The type of animal horn used to prepare the *Mpaka* will depend on the particular *Congo Spirit Deity*. The *Mpaka* in itself is a miniature *Spirit Nganga* which can be transported easily. The *Mpaka* holds the complete Mysteries of a particular *Congo Spirit*. The *Mpaka* contains the complete *"Spiritual DNA Coding"* of that particular spirit and by using the *Mpaka,* the Congo Priest can duplicate and give birth to another spirit of the same type without all of the other Mysteries being present contained and found in the Nganga of the *Aje Spirits*. A Congo Priest (Mayombero) can take his *Mpaka* anywhere in the world and by using the Mysteries contained within it rebuild his Nganga. The *Mpaka* is the "third eye" and the "ears of the Congo Spirits". When a glass mirror is placed on the open end of the *Mpaka* to cover the magical ingredients within it, it is termed "*Vititi Menso*" meaning the "all seeing eye". With the *Mpaka,* a Congo Priest can duplicate an unlimited amount of prepared Spirit Ngangas of the same exact spirit. After this *Mpaka* has been prepared for the *Aje Spirits it* should be completely covered in strands of black, red and white beads. When you are doing any type of sacred rituals for the *Aje Spirits* outside of the traditional Congo Munanzo religious shrine area such as in the Mountains, Forest, Cemetery or River, you only need to bring the *Mpaka* and the *Mbele* along with you if you will be feeding them or even invoking them. The *Mpaka* makes it spiritually easy to transport the complete Congo Spirits with you without having to bring along all of their other Mysteries (sacred items) with you. *(the Nganga of the Aje Spirits, the Ozun De Aje and the Ozain De Aje).*

ITEMS NECESSARY

1. *ONE LARGE BULL'S HORN (1 to 2 1/2 FEET IN LENGTH)*
2. *THREE LIGHTNING STONES*
3. *ONE SMALL OBLONG STONE FROM THE TOP OF A MOUNTAIN*
4. *THREE QUARTZ CRYSTALS*
5. *MAGNETIC SAND*
6. *IRON OXIDATE POWDER*
7. *THREE SMALL METEORITE STONES*
8. *NINE PIECES OF SILVER*
9. *NINE PIECES OF GOLD*
10. *NINE PIECES OF COPPER*
11. *NINE PIECES OF BRONZE*
12. *NINE PIECES OF TIN*
13. *NINE PIECES OF IRON*
14. *COINS FROM AROUND THE WORLD*
15. *DIRT FROM 121 TOMBS OF WOMEN*
16. *DIRT FROM THE MOUNTAINS/HILLS*
17. *DIRT FROM THE OCEAN'S EDGE*
18. *DIRT FROM THREE CHURCHES*
19. *SAND FROM THREE CROSSROADS*
20. *DIRT FROM A FIELD*
21. *DIRT FROM A FOREST*
22. *DIRT FROM THREE GATES*
23. *DIRT FROM THE INITIATES HOUSE (4 CORNERS OF THE PROPERTY)*
24. *ONE VENOMOUS SNAKE (Dried)*
25. *ONE BAT (Dried)*
26. *POWDERED BONES FROM 121 BIRDS OF FLIGHT*
27. *ONE GALLON OF OCEAN WATER*
28. *ONE GALLON OF RIVER WATER*
29. *ONE QUART MAY RAIN WATER* (OPTIONAL)
30. *POWDERED HUMAN BONES* (FEMALE)
31. *TWENTY-ONE PALOS IN POWDERED FORM*
32. *TOOTH FROM A TIGER*
33. (3) *TEETH FROM A DECEASED HUMAN* (FEMALE)
34. *TONGUE AND EYES FROM A ROOSTER (Dried)*

35. *TONGUE AND EYES FROM A GUINEA HEN (Dried)*
36. *TONGUE AND EYES FROM A PARROT (Dried)*
37. *EYES FROM AN OWL (Dried)*
38. *EYES FROM A RAVEN (Dried)*
39. *EYES FROM A WOLF (Dried)*
40. *BONES FROM A VULTURE (Dried)*
41. *POWDERED SPIDERS (Dried)*
42. *POWDERED DRIED LEAVES FROM A CEIBA TREE*
43. *POWDERED DRIED PALM LEAFS*
44. *POWDERED DRIED OAK LEAFS*
45. *DRIED ROOTS FROM AN OAK TREE*
46. *DEER HORN POWDER*
47. *RATTLE FROM A RATTLESNAKE*
48. *POWDERED CHAMELEON LIZARD (Dried)*
49. *21 FRESH HERBS* (SACRED TO THE SPIRIT OZAIN)
50. *DRIED SQUASH SEEDS*
51. *LIQUID MERCURY*

52. *FINGER NAIL CUTTINGS, TOE NAIL CUTTINGS AND BODY HAIR FROM VARIOUS PARTS OF THE BODY OF THE OWNER OF THE AJE SPIRIT NGANGA WRAPED IN A RED CLOTH BUNDLE. THE INSIDE OF THE RED CLOTH SHOULD HAVE THE SPIRIT SIGNATURE OF THE AJE SPIRITS PAINTED ON ONE SIDE.*

53. *ONE ROUND MIRROR (THE MIRROR MUST FIT PERFECTLY INTO THE OPEN END OF THE BULL'S HORN)*

54. *FAST DRY CEMENT*

LIVE ANIMALS NECESSARY

(2) BLACK ROOSTERS

PREPARATION

1. In a large mixing bowl, prepare an *Omiero* using the *Fresh Herbs.* Use the *Grains of Paradise, Ocean Water, River Water, May Rain Water, Holy Water* from a *Church* and the *Milk* from one *Coconut* in the preparation of the *Omiero.* After you have prepared the *Omiero,* place the *Lightning Stone,* the *Mountain Stone,* the (3) *Quartz Crystals,* the *Coins,* the *Silver,* the *Gold,* the *Tin,* the *Copper,* the *Bronze,* the *Iron Pieces* and the *Bull's Horn* into the *Omiero* mixture to soak and remain for 24 hours. Light a large seven day *White Religious Glass Candle* and set it next to the bowl of *Omiero* to give light and blessing to the items that will go into the *Mpaka (Bull's Horn).*

2. After the 24 hours, remove the *Bull's Horn.*

3. Take a mouthful of *Rum* and spray it directly into the empty *Bull's Horn.*

4. Light a *Cigar* and blow it directly into the *Bull's Horn.*
5.After you have finished this procedure, the *Bull's Horn* which will be housing the magical elements of the *Aje Spirits* has been baptized and is now ready to receive the other sacred items.

6. Pour the *Mercury* into the bottom of the empty *Bull's Horn.*

7. In a large bucket, mix all of the *Dirts, Magnetic Sand, Powdered Herbs* and *Palos,* the *Powdered Human Bone Powder,* the *Iron Oxidate Powder,* the *Powdered Spiders,* the *Powdered Bats,* the *Powdered Snakes,* the *Powdered Chameleons,* the *Powdered Spiders,* the *Deer Horn Powder, Powdered Bones of 121 Birds, Tooth* from a *Tiger, Human Teeth, Tongue* and *Eyes* from a *Rooster, Tongue* and *Eyes* from a *Guinea Hen, Tongue* and *Eyes* from a *Parrot, Eyes* from an *Owl, Eyes* from a *Raven, Eyes* from a *Wolf, Vulture Bones, Powdered Plants* and *Roots.*

8. After you have mixed all of these magical ingredients together, pour in some of the *Omiero* mixture into the bucket containing the magical mixture of ingredients and make a thick past like mixture.

9. Add a small amount of the past mixture into the empty *Bull's Horn* and firmly pack it down.

10. Place the *Lightning Stone* into the *Bull's Horn*.

11. Add some more of the paste mixture into the *Bull's Horn*.

12. Place the *Quartz Crystals* into the *Bull's Horn* and cover with the paste mixture.

13. Place all of the *Coins, Gold, Silver, Bronze, Iron, Tin* and *Copper Pieces* into the *Bull's Horn* and cover with the paste mixture.

14. Place the *Red Cloth Bundle* which will contain the new initiate's personal items, the *Rattle from the Rattlesnake,* the *Bat* and the *Dried Venomous Snake* into the *Horn* and then cover all the items with all of the rest of the remaining paste mixture. Firmly pack all of these ingredients into the *Bull's Horn*.

15. Feed the *Aje Spirit's Mpaka* the blood from one *Rooster* and allow it to remain for 3 hours.

16. After the 3 hours, light a white candle and allow the *Wax* to drip over the top of the *Bull's Horn* and to completely cover the open end of the it.
17. Place the *Mirror* onto the top of the *Bull's Horn* on top of the *Wax*.

18. After the *Wax* has dried with the *Mirror* embedded in it, seal the *Mirror* onto the *Bull's Horn* with the fast dry cement with a good area of the *Mirror* showing.

19. After the cement has dried, feed the *Aje Spirit's Mpaka* again with the blood of the other *Rooster*.

The Mpaka of the Aje Spirits.

HOW TO PREPARE THE OZUN DE AJE (ORERE)

The *Ozun of the Aje Spirits* is another important key element of the *Aje Spirits Nganga*. The *Ozun of the Aje Spirits* is the *"spiritual antenna"* of the *Aje Spirits Nganga*. The *Ozun of the Aje Spirits* allows these powerful spiritual entities to receive and send clear spiritual messages from the spiritual dimension where their dwell to our dimension thus being able to create a very powerful high level of spiritual vibration and magical energy wavelengths to assist the Congo Priest with their spiritual requests to accomplish any and all of their magical spells. The *Ozun De Aje* is placed directly behind the *Aje Spirits Nganga*. Without the *Ozun De Aje,* it is unlikely that the supernatural energy that is spiritually channeled from the *World of the Aje Spirits* would be stable enough to be able to be harnessed and used for magical power by the Congo Priest.

ITEMS NECESSARY

1. *ONE LARGE CLAY CERAMIC POT (TALL)*
2. *ONE LARGE NATURAL WOOD POLE /* STICK (3 - 9 FEET TALL)
3. *ONE METAL OZUN DE ORISHA*
4. *ONE VERY SMALL LIGHTNING STONE*
5. *ONE VERY SMALL QUARTZ CRYSTAL*
6. *MAGNETIC SAND*
7. *ONE VERY SMALL METEORITE STONE*
8. *DEER HORN POWDER*
9. *ONE PIECE OF SILVER*
10. *ONE PIECE OF GOLD*
11. *ONE PIECE OF COPPER*
12. *ONE PIECE OF BRONZE*
13. *ONE PIECE OF TIN*
14. *ONE PIECE OF IRON*
15. (121) *SEEDS FROM VARIOUS PLANTS*
16. (21) *PEONIA SEEDS*
17. *DIRT FROM* (121) *TOMBS OF WOMEN*

18. *VENOMOUS SNAKES* (POWDERED)
19. *BATS* (POWDERED)
20. *POWDERED BONES FROM* (121) *BIRDS OF FLIGHT*
21. *POWDERED HERBS* (9) *SACRED TO THE AJE SPIRITS*
22. *ONE POUND OF POWDERED DRIED LEAVES FROM A CEIBA TREE*
23. *ONE POUND OF POWDERED DRIED PALM LEAFS*
24. *POWDERED DRIED OAK TREE LEAFS*
25. *TWENTY-ONE POWDERED PALOS*
26. *POWDERED ACHE DE SANTO*
27. *THIRTY-SIX COINS FROM AROUND THE WORLD*
28. *DIRT FROM NINE TOMBS OF WOMEN*
29. *DIRT FROM THE MOUNTAINS/HILLS*
30. *DIRT FROM THE OCEAN'S EDGE*
31. *DIRT FROM THREE CHURCHES*
32. *SAND FROM THREE CROSSROADS*
33. *DIRT FROM A FIELD*
34. *DIRT FROM A FOREST*
35. *DIRT FROM THREE GATES*
36. *DIRT FROM THE INITIATES HOUSE (4 CORNERS OF THE PROPERTY)*
37. *FAST DRY CEMENT*
38. *LIQUID MERCURY*

LIVE ANIMALS NEEDED

1. ONE BLACK ROOSTER
2. ONE GUINEA HEN

PREPARATION

1. In a large mixing bowl, prepare an *Omiero* using the *(21) Herbs,* the *Grains of Paradise, Ocean Water, River Water, Holy Water a Church* and the *Coconut Water* in the preparation of the *Omiero*. After you have prepared the *Omiero,* place the *Metal Ozun* into the *Omiero* liquid mixture along with the *Lightning Stone, Quartz Crystal, Meteorite Stone, Silver, Gold, Copper, Bronze, Tin, Iron*, and the *Coins*. Light a *White Candle* next to the bowl and allow the items to remain for a 24 hour period of time.

2. Draw the sacred *Spirit Signature* of the *Aje Spirits* on the bottom inside of the tall *Ceramic Pot* using the *Black* and *Red Paint.*

3. Seal the symbol using *Virgin Candle Wax.*

4. Take a mouthful of *Rum* and spray it into the tall large *Ceramic Pot.*

5. Light a *Cigar* and blow the smoke into the tall large *Ceramic Pot.*

6. In a large bucket, mix all of the *Dirts* together with the *21 Powdered Palos,* the *Human Bone Powder,* the *Deer Horn Powder, Magnetic Sand, Powdered Bats, Powdered Venomous Snakes, Powdered Herbs, Powdered Leafs* from a *Ceiba Tree, Powdered Leafs* from a *Palm Tree, Powdered Leafs* from an *Oak Tree,* and the *Ache De Santo*. MIX WELL.

7. After you have mixed all of the items together, pour in some of the *Omiero* mixture into the bucket containing the *Dirt* mixture and make a thick past mixture.

8. Remove the *Ozun* from the *Omiero* liquid, dry and then attach it to one flat end of the *Wood Pole.*

9. Open up the *Metal Ozun* by unscrewing it and adding as much of the paste mixture as possible into it along with the *Lightning Stone, Meteorite Stone, Silver, Gold, Copper, Bronze, Tin, Iron, (121) Seeds*, and the *Peonia Seeds.*

10. Once you have packed the *Ozun,* then seal shut with the metal top of the *Ozun.*

11. Mix the fast dry cement to the remaining *Dirt* and powder paste like mixture.

12. Place the *Wood Pole* with the *Ozun De Aje* attached to it into the center of the tall *Ceramic Pot* and then pour in the cement mixture around the pole all the way up to the rim of the tall *Ceramic Pot.*

13. Hold the *Wood Pole* carefully until the cement mixture has dried.

14. The pole containing the *Ozun De Aje* should now be able to stand up on its own.

15. After the cement has dried, feed the *Ozun of the Nganga* with the blood of a *Rooster* and a *Guinea Hen.*

16. After the *Ozun De Aje* is finished, set it next to the *Aje Spirit Nganga* along with a *White Candle.*

FEED THE "OZUN DE AJE" EVERY TIME YOU FEED THE AJE SPIRIT NGANGA.

A picture of the Aje Spirit Mysteries.

HOW TO PREPARE THE OZAIN OF THE AJE SPIRITS (TITILLERO)

The *Ozain of the Aje Spirits* is another magical key element to the successful manisfestation of the *Aje Spirits.* The *Ozain De Aje* is prepared inside of a dried hollow gourd (Guiro). This gourd is also known in the Caribbean as a Calabash Gourd. The *Ozain De Aje* is filled with a variety of magical items. The *Ozain de Aje* is hung from the pole of the *Ozun De Aje* by a string. The *Ozain De Aje* is an important part and element of the completed nganga of the *Aje Spirits* because it is used to keep the energy of the spirit balanced and magically active. The *Ozain De Aje* is a very powerful magical amulet to ward off evil and spiritual attacks of witchcraft against you from your occult enemies. The *Ozain De Aje* can be covered in strands of beads in the color combinations of Red, Black and White after it has been completely prepared. The sacred Mysteries of the *Ozain De Aje* must be fed each and every time that you feed the *Aje Spirits* blood from any sacrificed animals to them in exchange for their blessings.

ITEMS NECESSARY

1. *ONE LARGE HOLLOW EMPTY GOURD/CALABASH WITH STRING ATTACHED*
2. *ONE VERY SMALL LIGHTNING STONE*
3. *ONE VERY SMALL QUARTZ CRYSTAL*
4. *MAGNETIC SAND*
5. *ONE VERY SMALL METEORITE STONE*
6. *DEER HORN POWDER*
7. *ONE PIECE OF SILVER*
8. *ONE PIECE OF GOLD*
9. *ONE PIECE OF COPPER*
10. *ONE PIECE OF BRONZE*
11. *ONE PIECE OF TIN*
12. *ONE PIECE OF IRON*

13. *ONE HUNDRED - TWENTY-ONE SEEDS FROM VARIOUS PLANTS*
14. (21) *PEONIA SEEDS*
15. *DIRT FROM TWENTY-ONE TOMBS OF WOMEN*
16. *VENOMOUS SNAKES* (POWDERED)
17. *BATS* (POWDERED)
18. *POWDERED BONES FROM* (121) *BIRDS OF FLIGHT*
19. *POWDERED HERBS* (9) *SACRED TO THE AJE SPIRITS*
20. *ONE POUND OF POWDERED DRIED LEAVES FROM A CEIBA TREE*
21. *ONE POUND OF POWDERED DRIED PALM LEAFS*
22. *POWDERED DRIED OAK TREE LEAFS*
23. *TWENTY-ONE POWDERED PALOS*
24. *POWDERED ACHE DE SANTO*
25. *THIRTY-SIX COINS FROM AROUND THE WORLD*
26. *DIRT FROM NINE TOMBS OF WOMEN*
27. *DIRT FROM THE MOUNTAINS/HILLS*
28. *DIRT FROM THE OCEAN'S EDGE*
29. *DIRT FROM THREE CHURCHES*
30. *SAND FROM THREE CROSSROADS*
31. *DIRT FROM A FIELD*
32. *DIRT FROM A FOREST*
33. *DIRT FROM THREE GATES*
34. *DIRT FROM THE INITIATES HOUSE* (4 CORNERS OF THE PROPERTY)
35. *LIQUID MERCURY*

PREPARATION

1. Blow *Cigar Smoke* and *Rum* into the empty *Gourd /Calabash* to consecrate it.

2. Using *Black* and *Red Paint,* paint the sacred *Spirit Signature* of the *Aje Spirits* on the inside bottom of the hollow *Gourd/Calabash.*

3. Place all of the ingredients listed into the *Gourd/Calabash.*

4. Firmly pack all the ingredients into the *Gourd/Calabash.*

5. Pour *Omiero* into the *Gourd/ Calabash*

6. Hang the prepared *"Ozain De Aje"* from the *Pole of the Ozun De Aje.*

7. Feed the *Ozain De Aje* the blood from a *Black Rooster,* a *Grey Pigeon* and a *Guinea Hen.*

HOW TO PREPARE THE MBELE OF THE AJE SPIRITS

The *Mbele* is the sacred *Machete of the Aje Spirits.* Once it has been ritually prepared it is then placed next to the *Aje Spirits Nganga* until ready to use in summoning these powerful spiritual entities. The *Mbele of the Aje Spirits* is magically used to send off the *Aje Spirits* to do your bidding by using *"Fula".* The *Mbele De Aje Spirits* is also used by a Congo Priest in the same way that a sorcerer would use a magician's magic wand.

<u>ITEMS NECESSARY</u>

ONE NEW MACHETE (24 INCHES IN LENGTH)

PREPARATION

1. In a large mixing bowl, prepare an *Omiero* using the *(21) Herbs*, the *Grains of Paradise, Ocean Water, River Water, Holy Water a Church* and the *Coconut Water* in the preparation of the *Omiero*. After you have prepared the *Omiero*, place the *Mbele (Machete)* into the *Omiero* liquid and light a *White Candle* next to the bowl and allow the *Mbele* to remain for a 24 hour period of time.

2. After the 24 hour period, remove the *Mbele* and allow it to dry off naturally.

3. Draw the sacred *Spirit Signature* of the *Mbele* of the *Aje Spirits* on the *Mbele* using *White Paint*.

4. Take a mouthful of *Rum* and spray it onto the *Mbele* to consecrate it.

5. Light a *Cigar* and blow the smoke onto the *Mbele* to consecrate it.

6. Feed the *Mbele of the Aje Spirits* the blood from a *Black Rooster*.

7. After feeding the *Mbele of the Aje*, set it next to the *Aje Spirits Nganga* until ready to ritually use to invoke and to summon them.

HOW TO PRESENT THE AJE SPIRITS INITIATION CEREMONY

The *Aje Spirits Initiation Ceremony* is one of the most beautiful ceremonies of the Congo religion. When an individual receives this initiation the *"Divine Universal Forces"* are called to descend down upon the ritual to bestow to the new initiate the *"spiritual right"* to walk in the invisible world of the *Aje Spirits* with authority and command. This sacred ceremony links the new initiate to the invisible world of the powerful *Aje Spirits* who are the rightful owners of and who govern the *Universal Laws of the (4) Elements of Earth*. These *(4) Elements* are *Air, Water, Earth* and *Fire*. When the new initiate receives this initiation they will be given the authority of how to use the "secret keys of knowledge" to be able to spiritually work with these *(4) Universal Elements* which are necessary and are involved in all spiritual or magical manifestations. All *(4) Universal Elements* are considered and believed to be *"Universal Elements of Creation."* Therefore in your magical work of reality creation, these *(4) Universal Elements* must be used for your magical manifestations to be complete. The reason for any failure of magical manifestation is only because of misalignment in any of these *(4) Universal Elements*. The number (4) is the *"number of creation."* The more you know about the universe, the better you can create powerful magic.

The first Universal Element which is governed by the *Aje Spirits* is *Air*. This element represents intention. Wind or air is the mental plane of reality. It is the plane of pure information or data. In using the Universal Element of wind, you are dealing with pure thought. In this realm, you can use visualization, affirmation and pure intent which can also be referred to as goal setting. These three activities take place on the mental plane. You can use any of these three or all of them together. Have an intent or goal to achieve, visualize the outcome and affirm that it is materialized.

The second Universal Element which is governed by the *Aje Spirits* is *Water*. This element represents emotion. Water is the emotional or astral plane of reality. It is the plane of desire. Whatever you feel manifests first on this plane. In this realm, you can use the act of generating emotion for manifestation. This is where you get the feeling of having already attained your desire. Energy is needed for creation and your feeling is the energy. Feelings of peace, joy and gratitude provides the energy for manifesting like conditions. Your feeling is resonance and attraction.

The third Universal Element which is governed by the *Aje Spirits* is *Earth*. This element represents action. Earth is the ethereal and physical plane of reality. It is the plane of materialization. Many a times, your desires already exist in the mental and emotional plane of reality, but you are required to take action to complete the manifestation process. Inspired action is the avenue by which ideas are brought into form on the material plane. Action is what enables you to be part of the manifestation process. The joy is in experiencing creation happening through you.

The forth Universal Element which is governed by the *Aje Spirits* is *Fire*. This element represents righteousness. Fire is the soul or causal plane of reality. It is the plane of divine will. If your intentions are in alignment with the intents of your higher self, then it has allowance to manifest. You may have visualized, felt your desire as a reality and taken inspired action but still haven't experienced the manifestation of your desire. That is because according to righteousness, it is not the right time or setting. Your higher self is handling the entire process of unfoldment.

Although there are four Universal Elements of creation, there is also a fifth one by which all four arises from. The fifth Universal Element is spirit (emptiness or void). It is not really empty or void but it is simply pure, undefined energy. This energy is consciousness which is differentiated into all four aspects of itself which are intent, emotion, action and higher intent. One must bring the mind to a state of emptiness by clearing all thoughts except for one, which is the intent. From a state of single mindedness, your intention has great clarity. All four Universal Elements of your magical desires and or manifestation must be working in harmony with one another for it to succeed. You must visualize and affirm what you desire instead of what you do not desire. You must feel the joy of having your desire instead of the fear of lacking it. You must do everything in alignment with your intent instead of acting in ways that are opposite to it. You must also detach and trust in divine order and divine timing of your higher self to arrange the unfoldment. With the four Universal Elements in spiritual alignment with the *Aje Spirits,* you cannot fail. There is also another aspect of righteousness which is karma. Virtuous deeds will be recompensed by desirable gains while deeds that lack virtue will attract retribution. The great Universe is a mirror. What you do will be reflected back to you. Give and it shall be given back to you. When you express abundance by giving to others for their gain, the Universe will reflect your virtuous deeds with greater abundance. Your desires have more power to manifest when you have generated a store of good karma for yourself. Within righteousness is also your sense of deserving. If you want something but do not believe that you deserve to have it, your conflicting belief will repel your desire away from you. If you want to receive what you desire, you must believe that you have the right to have it. The why behind your intention is also your fire to achieve it. When you have a purpose for achieving something, you will be driven towards it. Fire is what supplements your thoughts, emotions and actions with the energy to keep on persisting. The purpose behind an intent also determines its power to manifest. When you desire something for the greatest good of yourself and the universe, your intention is highly imbued with virtue.

Any intent that is directly aligned with the nature of the universal mind will be aided by the entire Universe itself. That is because you are not just having a personal intent but you are taking on the intents of the Universe. Intents that are love based come from a holistic point of view. If Nzambi (God) is for you, who can be against you? When something isn't happening for you, use wisdom to consider what might be a better intention to have? The Universe is always working everything for your highest good, and it is always giving you what you really want. The Universe is your total self and therefore you are never denied your true will. Your magical manifestations can also happen faster and more easily when you have opportunities and contacts set up on the physical plane. Success sets the stage for further success. Everything plays a part in Universal Spiritual completion. Without a new initiate undergoing this very important initiation by which you make a pact with the *Aje Spirits* and establish a peaceful relationship with these powerful entities you will not be able to accomplish any magical goals. If a new initiate does not undergo a ritual with the *Aje Spirits* which binds us to their world the Congo magician will find it almost impossible to achieve their magical desires with accuracy. Because these powerful entities are naturally found within of nature the *Aje Spirits Initiation Ceremony* must be done completely outdoors and in open nature. The best time to receive this initiation would be on a "*New Moon*" or a "*Full Moon*". If you receive this initiation and make a spiritual pact "spiritual truce" with them nothing that you do magically will be impossible. If a new initiate does not undergo this initiation with the *Aje Spirits* you will be always be plagued with the perils of life. These powerful *Aje Spirits* which are more than often times overlooked because out of fear or ignorance by initiates of Congo religion must be appeased first in order to be able to gain control and spiritual command within the invisible spiritual world. If you have already received this powerful initiation and it was not done like the following ritual you should do it again to make sure that you have a firm stable spiritual balanced relationship between the *Aje Spirits* and the *Universal Elemental Forces of Air, Water, Earth* and *Fire*.

PART I

The first part of this initiation begins at the *Cemetery* (*CAMPO SANTO*) to give honor and thanks of the spirits who dwell there. The powerful *Aje Spirits* although mainly found in nature are also connected to and do govern various magical aspects of the *Cemetery*. This ceremony establishes a spiritual connection to the World of the *Aje Spirits* that will be able to assist you with your future magical endeavours.

PLEASE NOTE THAT ANY OF THE CEREMONIAL TIMES OF DAY LISTED IN THIS SACRED INITIATION RITUAL CAN ALSO BE DONE IN THE DAYLIGHT HOURS.

IF YOU ARE PREPARING THE SACRED AJE MYSTERIES FOR YOURSELF THEN YOU CAN MODIFY THE RITUAL TO FIT YOUR NEEDS.

1. Take the individual who will be receiving the "*Aje Spirits*" to the *Cemetery* at *9 PM*.

2. Find a *Grave* that has an upright *Tombstone* shaped like a *Cross*.

3. Take *(4) White Candles* and attach them to the *Tombstone* using melted *Wax*.

4. Place one *Candle* at the top of the *Cross*, another *Candle* at both sides of the *Cross* and at its base in the ground in front of the *Cross Tombstone*.

5. Light all *(4) Candles*.

6. Pour liquor over the *Tomb*, blow smoke on the *Tomb* and place (9) pennies at the base of the *Tomb*.

7. Draw the *Spirit Signature* of the *Aje Spirits* using *Cascarilla Powder* on the ground. The *Spirit Signature* should be large

enough so that the individual can stand on top of it. Blindfold the individual.

8. Light a *White Candle* and present it to the following areas of the new initiate; top of their head, their feet, their left shoulder, their right shoulder, the top of their head once again, the back of the left shoulder, the back of the right shoulder and the back of both legs.

9. Afterwards, give the *Candle* to the individual in their hands and ask them to pray silently to Nzambi (*God)*, to the *Aje Spirits,* to their *Eggun (Ancestors)* and to the Nkisi (*Congo Spirits)* for blessings.

10. Light a *Cigar* and blow the smoke over the body of the individual. (3 times)

11. Take a mouthful of *Rum* and spray it all over the body of the individual. (3 times)

12. After the individual has finished praying, take the *White Candle* and stick it into the ground near the *Tomb* that has a headstone in the form of a *Cross.*

13. Take a *Black Hen* & a *Black Rooster* and spiritually cleanse the individual from head to toe.

14. Give the *Black Hen* & the *Black Rooster* one at a time to the individual and tell them to hold it up to their forehead and pray to Nzambi (*God)*, to the *Aje Spirits,* to their *Eggun (Ancestors)* and to the Nkisi (*Congo Spirits)* for blessings.

15. After they have finished praying, sacrifice the *Hen*, the *Rooster* and feed the blood around the grave area which the individual is standing.

16. Place the body of the *Hen* & the *Rooster* near the *Candle* and pour *Bee's Honey* over it.

17. Light a *Cigar* and blow the smoke over the body of the individual. (3 times)

18.Take a mouthful of *Rum* and spray it over the body of the individual. (3 times)

19. Give the new initiate a bundle of *Fresh Flowers* and have them kneel down in front of the *Cross Tombstone*. The individual prays and then sets the flowers next to the body of the *Rooster* along with also pouring sweet fragrance woman's perfume all over the ritual area.

PART II

1. Take the individual who will be receiving the *"AJE SPIRITS"* to the *River at 12 Midnight.*

2. Draw the *Spirit Signature* of the *AJE SPIRITS* using *Cascarilla Powder* on the ground near the river bank. The *Spirit Signature* should be large enough so that the individual can stand on top of it. Blindfold the individual.

3. Light a *White Candle* and present it to the following areas of the individual; top of their head, both of their feet, both left & right front shoulders, the top of their head once again, the back of both left and right shoulders, the back of both legs.

4. Afterwards, give the *Candle* to the individual in their hands and ask them to pray silently to Nzambi *(God)*, to the *Aje Spirits,* to their *Eggun (Ancestors)* and to the Nkisi *(Congo Spirits)* for blessings.

5. Light a *Cigar* and blow the smoke over the body of the individual. (3 times)

6. Take a mouthful of *Rum* and spray it over the body of the individual. (3 times)

7. After the individual has finished praying, take the *White Candle* and stick it into the ground near the side of the river in the damp soil.

8. Take a *Black Hen* and a *Black Rooster* and spiritually cleanse the individual from head to toe.

9. Give the *Black Hen* and the *Black Rooster* one at a time to the individual and tell them to hold it up to their forehead and pray to the powerful *Aje Spirits* to seek their blessings.

10. After they have finished praying, sacrifice both the *Rooster* and the *Hen* and feed the blood to all of the sacred items of the *Aje Spirits* and also around the area which the individual is standing and into the river water.

11. Place the body of both the *Rooster* and the *Hen* near the candle and pour bee's honey over it and into the river.

12. Begin the *Rompemiento* (spiritual cleansing) by tearing the individual's clothes off and then throw the torn clothes into the river to be swept away.

13. Light a *Cigar* and blow the smoke over the body of the individual. (3 times)

14. Take a mouthful of rum and spray it over the body of the individual. (3 times)

15. Lead the individual by the hand into the *River* to bathe using *African Black Soap* and a handful of *(9) Fresh Herbs* to scrub the negative vibration off their bodies to prepare for the *Aje Spirits Initiation Ceremony.*

16. When the individual has finished, assist the individual to place on a set of complete *New White Clothes.*

PART III - THE INITIATION

1. The individual who will be receiving the initiation of the *Aje Spirits* will be blind folded and led to the ceremonial area that will be lit up with candles.

2. All of the individual's sacred items that they will be receiving *(Aje Spirit Nganga, Ozun De Aje, Mpaka De Aje, Mbele De Aje and the Ozain De Aje)* will be placed and set up next to to river.

3. The *Congo Priest* presiding over the initiation ceremony will then begin the initiation ritual by first reciting the *Congo* prayers to the *Aje Spirits* to grant safe passage and protection to all the members present who are attending the initiation ritual ceremony.

4. The *Congo Priest* will then start the initiation ceremony and to invoke the *Aje Spirits* by saying the following:

PRIEST RECITES:

We invoke the powers of the Aje Spirits, the Mothers of the Sacred Marketplace, The Mothers of Invisibility, The Mothers of the (4) Universal Elemental Forces (Earth, Water, Fire and Air) . - Sala Malekun, Malekun Sala -

GROUP RECITES:

Sala Malekun, Malekun Sala

PRIEST RECITES:

We have come here tonight on this most sacred day to call upon the Aje Spirits, The Divine Mothers of the Night to grant us the power and the connection to deliver the "Sacred Word." Cover us with your Divine Protective Light and Protect us from all Evil and deliver us from our Enemies. Our Enemies are your Enemies and Your Enemies are Our Enemies.

GROUP RECITES:

Sala Malekun, Malekun Sala

PRIEST RECITES:

O Divine Mothers, Aje. We invoke you from the North, South, East and the West to hear our prayers and to come from where you live and from where you are.

GROUP RECITES:

Sala Malekun, Malekun Sala

PRIEST RECITES:

We have not come here tonight to challenge you or to make war and fight with you, because we know that we would not win.

GROUP RECITES:

Sala Malekun, Malekun Sala

PRIEST RECITES:

We have brought you the light of the sacred candles so you will light our roads in darkness. We have brought you the smell of sweet smelling incense to sweeten our lives. All of these things in honor of your great wisdom, your divine spirit and for who you are. (you should be burning sweet smelling powdered incense with powdered Oak Leafs added to it)

GROUP RECITES:

Sala Malekun, Malekun Sala.

PRIEST RECITES:

We call upon Nzambi the Creator of the Heavens and the Earth to witness this sacred ritual. Sala Malekun, Malekun Sala, We call upon Gonda (the Congo God of the Moon) to witness this sacred ritual. Sala Malekun, Malekun Sala, We call upon our Ancestors who are kneeling at the Foot of Nzambi (God) in Light to witness this ritual. Sala Malekun, Malekun Sala We call upon the Spirit Exu, the Divine Gate

Keeper, to witness this ritual Sala Malekun, Malekun Sala We call upon the Congo Spirit Ozain, the Keeper of the Mystical and Magical Secrets of the Divine Aje Spirits to witness this ritual Sala Malekun, Malekun Sala We call upon the Congo Spirits to witness this ritual and to bestow their blessings to all present here and to (say the name of the new initiate) who is knocking at your divine cosmic door of sacred knowledge. Sala Malekun, Malekun Sala

PRIEST:

Do you (say the name of the new initiate) swear on your blood and on your life that you will never reveal any part of this ceremony to anyone after this evening on this most sacred and holy of all days.

NEW INITIATE RESPONDS:

I swear on my blood and my life to never reveal this ceremony to anyone.

PRIEST:

Do you (say the name of the new initiate) swear on your blood and your life to promise that you will always remain loyal and true to this Congo Munanzo (say the same of your Congo Munanzo) and to defend its honor even if it means your life?

NEW INITIATE RESPONDS:

I swear on my blood and my life to always remain loyal and true to this Congo Munanzo (say the same of your Congo Munanzo) and to defend its honor even if it means my own life?

PRIEST:

Do you (say the name of the new initiate) swear on your blood and your life that you will not and never regret what you are about to do in this sacred ceremony in the morning?

NEW INITIATE RESPONDS:

I swear on my blood and my life that I will never regret what I am about to do in this ceremony in the morning.

PRIEST RECITES:

SALA MALEKUN, MALEKUN SALA

CON LA BENDICION DE NZAMBI

SALA MALEKUN, MALEKUN SALA

NZAMBI NPONGA

NZAMBI ARRIBA

NZAMBI NTOTO

NZAMBI DE LOS CUATRO COSTADOS

SALA MALEKUN, MALEKUN SALA

CON LA BENDICION DE LOS ESPIRITUS AJE, LAS MADRES INVISIBLES DE LA NOCHE

SALA MALEKUN, MALEKUN SALA

CON LA BENDICION DE MIS FAMILIARES DE LOS ANTEPASADOS QUE ESTAN A LOS PIES DE NZAMBI

SALA MALEKUN, MALEKUN SALA

CON LA BENDICION DE LOS BRUJOS CONGOS ANTEPASADOS Y MIS GUIAS ESPIRITUALES QUE ESTAN A LOS PIES DE NZAMBI

SALA MALEKUN, MALEKUN SALA

CON LA BENDICION DE EXU REI, EL REY DE LOS CUATROS CAMINOS INFIERNOS

SALA MALEKUN, MALEKUN SALA

CON LA BENDICION DE EXU MAIORAL, EL REY DE EL MUNDO ASTRAL OSCURO

SALA MALEKUN, MALEKUN SALA

CON LA BENDICION DE EL ESPIRITU CONGO OZAIN

SALA MALEKUN, MALEKUN SALA

CON LA BENDICION DE EL ESPIRITU CONGO ABITA

SALA MALEKUN, MALEKUN SALA

CON LA BENDICION DE EL ESPIRITU CONGO LUKANKANSE

SALA MALEKUN, MALEKUN SALA

CON LA BENDICION DE EL ESPIRITU CONGO LUCERO

SALA MALEKUN, MALEKUN SALA

CON LA BENDICION DE EL ESPIRITU CONGO ZARABANDA

SALA MALEKUN, MALEKUN SALA

CON LA BENDICION DE EL ESPIRITU CONGO CABO RONDO

SALA MALEKUN, MALEKUN SALA

CON LA BENDICION DE EL ESPIRITU CONGO TIEMBLA TIERRA

SALA MALEKUN, MALEKUN SALA

CON LA BENDICION DE EL ESPIRITU CONGO SIETE RAYOS

SALA MALEKUN, MALEKUN SALA

CON LA BENDICION DE EL ESPIRITU CONGO BRAZO FUERTE

SALA MALEKUN, MALEKUN SALA

CON LA BENDICION DE EL ESPIRITU CONGO TIEMPO VIEJO

SALA MALEKUN, MALEKUN SALA

CON LA BENDICION DE EL ESPIRITU CONGO KOBAYENDE

SALA MALEKUN, MALEKUN SALA

CON LA BENDICION DE EL ESPIRITU CONGO NSAMBA NTALA

SALA MALEKUN, MALEKUN SALA

CON LA BENDICION DE EL ESPIRITU CONGO MADRE DE AGUA

SALA MALEKUN, MALEKUN SALA

CON LA BENDICION DE EL ESPIRITU CONGO MAMA SHOLAN

SALA MALEKUN, MALEKUN SALA

CON LA BENDICION DE EL ESPIRITU CONGO CENTELLE NDOKI

SALA MALEKUN, MALEKUN SALA

I CALL THE SPIRITS FROM THE NORTH
I CALL THE SPIRITS FROM THE SOUTH
I CALL THE SPIRITS FROM THE EAST
I CALL THE SPIRITS FROM THE WEST

I AM HERE YOUR SON/DAUGHTER (SAY YOUR CONGO INTIATION NAME) SUMMONING YOU TO COME FROM WHERE YOU ARE FROM YOUR WORLD TO MY WORLD. PLACE A RING OF PROTECTIVE LIGHT AROUND ME SO THAT MY ENEMIES WILL NOT SEE ME NOR HEAR WHAT IS ABOUT TO BE REVEALED HERE IN THIS CEREMONY. YOUR ENEMIES ARE MY ENEMIES AND MY ENEMIES ARE YOUR ENEMIES. I HAVE BROUGHT YOU LIGHT, SO THAT YOU WILL LIGHT MY ROADS IN DARKNESS. I ASK YOU THAT ALL OF THE GOOD THINGS IN MY LIFE. MY MONEY, MY HEALTH, MY BUSINESS ETC... THAT WERE TAKEN UNJUSTLY AND STOLEN FROM ME BY MY ENEMIES THAT YOU BRING ALL OF THE GOOD THINGS BACK TO ME AND TO MY HANDS AT THIS VERY MOMENT FOR HERE WE STAND TOGETHER TO FIGHT A COMMON ENEMY. (SAY THI S 9 TIMES) FOR YOUR ENEMIES ARE MY ENEMIES AND MY ENEMIES ARE YOUR ENEMIES. (SAY THIS 9 TIMES) I CALL UPON THE SPIRIT EXU THE KEEPER OF THE CROSSROADS TO OPEN UP THE ROADS OF COMMUNICATION BETWEEN YOUR WORLD AND MY WORLD TO CONNECT THE DIVINE FORCE WHICH BINDS MAN TO THE GREAT COSMOS. I ASK YOU HERE AND NOW THAT WHAT EVER MY ENEMIES HAVE DONE IN THE PAST, ARE PRESENTLY DOING TO ME OR PLAN TO DO TO ME IN THE FUTURE THAT YOU PUNISH THEM 9X9X9 AND BRING THEM TO THEIR KNEES. WHATEVER THEY HAVE DONE OR PLAN TO DO TO ME REVERSE IT BACK TO THEM IN THE NAME OF DIVINE JUSTICE 9X9X9 SO THEY WILL RELIQUISH WHATEVER HOLD THEY HAVE OVER ME AND BE ON THEIR WAY.

EXU BREAK MY ENEMIES (SAY 3 TIMES)

EXU BIND MY ENEMIES (SAY 3 TIMES)

EXU BLIND MY ENEMIES (SAY 3 TIMES)

EXU DESTROY MY ENEMIES (SAY 3 TIMES)

IN THE NAME OF THE GREAT UNIVERSAL FORCE I PRAY THIS TODAY. MAY YOU GRANT ENTRANCE TO (SAY THE NAME OF THE NEW INITIATE) INTO THE WORLD OF COLORED DARKNESS. SALA MALEKUN, MALEKUN SALA

5. The new initiate will then be asked to kneel down in front of the sacred items.

6. As the individual is kneeling down, place the prepared *Nganga of the Aje Spirits* into the individual's hands.

7. The Congo Priest will then continue the ceremony by singing a series of mambos to the Congo Spirits (or any sacred song to reflect your particular magical tradition) to call the powerful entities from the spirit world.

8. The Congo Priest will light a cigar and blow the smoke over the body of the individual and into the *Nganga of the Aje Spirits* as well as over all the other sacred items.

9. The Congo Priest will then take a mouthful of rum and spray it over the body of the individual and over all of the sacred items.

10. The Congo priest will then cleanse the body of individual with a live Rooster, Hen and a Pigeon.

11. The animals are then sacrificed and the blood poured directly into the *Nganga of the Aje Spirits* as well as to the other sacred items that the new initiate will be receiving.

12. Place the *Mbele De Aje (Machete)* on the ground directly in front of the new initiate pointing in their direction. The handle of the *Mbele* must be touching the *Mpaka* of the new initiate and the *Mpaka of the Aje* from the *Congo Munanzo.*

13. Carefully take "*Fula*" and line the *Spirit Signature* drawn on the *Mbele* with a very thin amount.

14. The Congo Priest then recites the following:

DIVINE MOTHERS, AJE,
BESTOW YOUR POWERS UPON (SAY THE NEW INITIATE'S NAME)

AJE BRILLUMBI NDOKI INFIERNO VIRA MUNDO

AJE BRILLUMBI NDOKI INFIERNO VIRA MUNDO

AJE BRILLUMBI NDOKI INFIERNO VIRA MUNDO

AJE BRILLUMBI NDOKI INFIERNO VIRA MUNDO

AJE BRILLUMBI NDOKI INFIERNO VIRA MUNDO

AJE BRILLUMBI NDOKI INFIERNO VIRA MUNDO

AJE BRILLUMBI NDOKI INFIERNO VIRA MUNDO

AJE BRILLUMBI NDOKI INFIERNO VIRA MUNDO

AJE BRILLUMBI NDOKI INFIERNO VIRA MUNDO

WHO IS THE GREATEST IN HEAVEN? NZAMBI
WHO IS THE GREATEST IN HEAVEN? NZAMBI
WHO IS THE GREATEST IN HEAVEN? NZAMBI

WHO ARE YOU? AJE
WHO ARE YOU? AJE
WHO ARE YOU? AJE

(SAY THE NAME OF THE NEW INITIATE)

RECEIVE THE DIVINE POWER AND BLESSINGS OF THE AJE SPIRITS.

15. After reciting this prayer, the "*fula*" is then carefully lighted using a cigar or candle starting from the handle of the "*Mbele*" that is touching the *Mpakas*.The *fula* should burn from the *Mpakas* towards the direction of the new initiate. By doing this the spiritual energy of the *Aje Spirits* that has gathered and descended upon the initiation ritual will freely flow towards and into the aura of the new initiate.

(PLEASE NOTE THAT YOU MAY USE VESTA POWDER IN PLACE OF USING THE TRADITIONAL "FULA" (GUN POWDER)

16. After the *Aje Spirits Initiation Ceremony* all of the items will be taken back to the Congo Munanzo where they will stay and remain for 21 days. After the 21 days the new initiate will be able to take the *Aje Spirits* to their residence and place them in their appropriate location which is always outdoors.

17. After the *Aje Spirits Initiation Ceremony,* the new initiate must sleep on the floor on a straw mat directly in front of the "*Congo Munanzo's Aje Spirits Shrine.*"

18. Following the *Aje Spirits Initiation Ceremony,* the new initiate will take a *Omiero Herbal Bath* consisting of (21) Herbs for three consecutive days at their residence.

THE AJE SPIRITS SHOULD ALWAYS HAVE A LIGHTED CANDLE NEXT TO THEM. THE AJE SPIRITS SHOULD BE KEPT IN A PRIVATE SECURE LOCATION IN YOUR BACK YARD. WHEN THE NEW INITIATE TAKES THEIR AJE SPIRITS TO THEIR RESIDENCE FOR THE FIRST TIME, THESE AJE SPIRITS MUST BE GIVEN ENTRANCE (ENTRADA ESPIRITUAL) BY THE TATA OF THE CONGO MUNANZO INTO THE NEW INITIATE'S HOME BY RITUALLY AND CEREMONIALLY FEEDING THEM THE BLOOD FROM A BLACK HEN, A BLACK ROOSTER, A GREY PIGEON, RUM, CIGAR SMOKE AND BEE'S HONEY.

CEMETERY RITUALS

A spiritual cleansing to remove witchcraft or the spirit of death from an individual.

<u>ITEMS NECESSARY</u>
ONE ROOSTER
FOUR BLACK CANDLES
HONEY
RED WINE
RUM
CIGAR
PEMBA

1. Dig a large hole in the ground at the base of a large tree.

2. Using pemba, draw the spirit signature of the Aje Spirits around the large hole and place the Mpaka of the Aje Spirits next to it. The hole will be directly in the center of the spirit signature.

3. Place the four white candles in all of the cardinal directions (north, south, east, west).

4. Light the candles.

5. Light the cigar and blow the smoke over the ritual area and directly into the hole.

6. Take a mouthful of rum and blow it over the ritual area and directly into the hole.

7. Invoke the Congo spirits using the traditional prayers.

8. If you do not know the prayers in Spanish/Congo then you can say it in English.

9. Cleanse yourself and the others who are present there with the rooster.

10. When you have finished, sacrifice the rooster and allow the blood to drip directly into the hole and directly on to the Mpaka of the Aje Spirits.

11. When the rooster is dead, place the body into the hole.

12. Pour honey over the body in the hole.

13. Wash your hands and the knife using fresh water and rum directly over the hole.

14. Pour red wine into the hole.

15. Using the four coconut shell chamalongo divination method, check to see if the offerings were accepted with blessings of the spirits.

16. If the spirits respond positive, cover the hole up with dirt and allow the candles to remain burning until completely finished.

17. Locate a tombstone in the cemetery in the shape of a cross and cleanse yourself with a purple candle and the place it at the foot of the tombstone and light.

It is also recommended that you light a sweet smelling or floral incense while doing the ritual.

A brass bell can also be used during the ritual. The Aje Spirits like the sound of ringing bells and all types of chimes. When they hear it they usually respond more favorabaly.

A spiritual cleansing to remove legal problems from around an individual.

<u>ITEMS NECESSARY</u>
ONE ROOSTER
FOUR WHITE CANDLES
HONEY
RED WINE
RUM
CIGAR
PEMBA

1. Dig a large hole in the ground at the base of a large tree.

2. Using pemba, draw the spirit signature of the Aje Spirits around the large hole and place the Mpaka of the Aje Spirits next to it. The hole will be directly in the center of the spirit signature.

3. Place the four white candles in all of the cardinal directions (North, South, East, West)

4. Light the candles.

5. Light the cigar and blow the smoke over the ritual area and directly into the hole.

6. Take a mouthful of rum and blow it over the ritual area and directly into the hole.

7. Invoke the Congo spirits using the traditional prayers.

8. If you do not know the prayers in Spanish/Congo then you can say it in English.

9. Cleanse yourself and the others who are present there with the rooster.

10. When you have finished, sacrifice the rooster and allow the blood to drip directly into the hole and directly on to the Mpaka of the Aje Spirits.

11. When the rooster is dead, place the body into the hole.

12. Pour honey over the body in the hole.

13. Wash your hands and the knife using fresh water and rum directly over the hole.

14. Pour red wine into the hole.

15. Using the four coconut shell chamalongo divination method, check to see if the offerings were accepted with blessings of the spirits.

16. If the spirits respond positive, cover the hole up with dirt and allow the candles to remain burning until completely finished.

It is also recommended that you light a sweet smelling or floral incense while doing the ritual.

A brass bell can also be used during the ritual. The Aje Spirits like the sound of ringing bells and all types of chimes. When they hear it they usually respond more favorabaly.

RAILROAD RITUALS

A spiritual cleansing to reverse witchcraft or negative vibrations and send it back to your enemies known and unknown.

<u>ITEMS NECESSARY</u>
ONE BLACK ROOSTER
TWO BLACK CANDLES & TWO GREEN CANDLES
HONEY
BEER
RUM
CIGAR
PEMBA

1. Dig a large hole in the ground at the railroad

2. Using pemba, draw the spirit signature of the Aje Spirits around the large hole and place the Mpaka of the Aje Spirits next to it. The hole will be directly in the center of the spirit signature.

3. Place the four candles in all of the cardinal directions (north, south, east, west)

4. Light the candles.

5. Light the cigar and blow the smoke over the ritual area and directly into the hole.

6. Take a mouthful of rum and blow it over the ritual area and directly into the hole.

7. Invoke the Congo spirits using the traditional prayers.

8. If you do not know the prayers in Spanish/Congo then you can say it in English.

9. Cleanse yourself and the others who are present there with the rooster.

10. When you have finished, sacrifice the rooster and allow the blood to drip directly into the hole and directly on to the Mpaka of the Aje Spirits.

11. When the rooster is dead, place the body into the hole.

12. Pour honey over the body in the hole.

13. Wash your hands and the knife using fresh water and rum directly over the hole.

14. Pour red wine into the hole.

15. Using the four coconut shell chamalongo divination method, check to see if the offerings were accepted with blessings of the spirits.

16. If the spirits respond positive, cover the hole up with dirt and allow the candles to remain burning until completely finished.

17. Invoke the Congo spirits using the traditional prayers.

18. If you do not know the prayers in Spanish/Congo then you can say it in English.

19. Cleanse yourself and the others who are present there with the rooster.

20. When you have finished, sacrifice the rooster and allow the blood to drip directly into the hole & over the railroad tracks.

21. When the rooster is dead, place the body into the hole.

22. Pour honey over the body in the hole.

23. Wash your hands and the knife using fresh water and rum directly over the hole.

24. Pour beer into the hole and over the railroad tracks.
25. Using the four coconut shell chamalongo divination method, check to see if the offerings were accepted with blessings of the spirits.

26. If the spirits respond positive, cover the hole up with dirt and allow the candles to remain burning until completely finished.

It is also recommended that you light a sweet smelling or floral incense while doing the ritual.

A brass bell can also be used during the ritual. The Aje Spirits like the sound of ringing bells and all types of chimes. When they hear it they usually respond more favorabaly.

RIVER RITUALS

A spiritual cleansing to remove obstacles in romance and love. Use this cleansing when you need luck in love.

<u>ITEMS NECESSARY</u>
ONE BROWN HEN
FOUR YELLOW CANDLES
HONEY
PINK CHAMPAGNE
RUM
CIGAR
PEMBA

1. Dig a large hole in the ground near the river.

2. Using pemba, draw the spirit signature of the Aje Spirits around the large hole and place the Mpaka of the Aje Spirits next to it. The hole will be directly in the center of the spirit signature.

3. Place the four yellow candles in all of the cardinal directions (North, South, East, West)

4. Light the candles.

5. Light the cigar and blow the smoke over the ritual area and directly into the hole.

6. Take a mouthful of rum and blow it over the ritual area and directly into the hole.

7. Invoke the Congo spirits using the traditional prayers.

8. If you do not know the prayers in Spanish/Congo then you can say it in English.

9. Cleanse yourself and the others who are present there with the brown hen.

10. When you have finished, sacrifice the hen and allow the blood to drip directly into the hole and directly on to the Mpaka of the Aje Spirits.

11. When the hen is dead, place the body into the hole.

12. Pour honey over the body in the hole and into the river.

13. Wash your hands and the knife using fresh water and rum directly over the hole.

14. Pour the pink champagne into the hole and river.

15. Using the four coconut shell chamalongo divination method, check to see if the offerings were accepted with blessings of the spirits.

16. If the spirits respond positive, cover the hole up with dirt and allow the candles to remain burning until completely finished.

It is also recommended that you light a sweet smelling or floral incense while doing the ritual.

A brass bell can also be used during the ritual. The Aje Spirits like the sound of ringing bells and all types of chimes. When they hear it they usually respond more favorabaly.

MOUNTAIN RITUALS

A spiritual cleansing to remove obstacles in your path that are blocking your wealth, money and financial prosperity.

ITEMS NECESSARY
ONE PIGEON
FOUR WHITE CANDLES
HONEY
RED WINE
RUM
CIGAR
PEMBA

1. Dig a large hole in the ground at the base of a large tree.

2. Using pemba, draw the spirit signature of the Aje Spirits around the large hole and place the Mpaka of the Aje Spirits next to it. The hole will be directly in the center of the spirit signature.

3. Place the four white candles in all of the cardinal directions (north, south, east, west)

4. Light the candles.

5. Light the cigar and blow the smoke over the ritual area and directly into the hole.

6. Take a mouthful of rum and blow it over the ritual area and directly into the hole.

7. Invoke the Congo spirits using the traditional prayers.

8. If you do not know the prayers in Spanish/Congo then you can say it in English.

9. Cleanse yourself and the others who are present there with the pigeon.

10. When you have finished, sacrifice the rooster and allow the blood to drip directly into the hole and directly on to the Mpaka of the Aje Spirits.

11. When the pigeon is dead, place the body into the hole.

12. Pour honey over the body in the hole.

13. Wash your hands using fresh water and rum directly over the hole.

14. Pour red wine into the hole.

15. Using the four coconut shell chamalongo divination method, check to see if the offerings were accepted with blessings of the spirits.

16. If the spirits respond positive, cover the hole up with dirt and allow the candles to remain burning until completely finished.

It is also recommended that you light a sweet smelling or floral incense while doing the ritual.

A brass bell can also be used during the ritual. The Aje Spirits like the sound of ringing bells and all types of chimes. When they hear it they usually respond more favorabaly.

FIELD RITUALS

A spiritual cleansing to remove both physical and spiritual sickness.

<u>ITEMS NECESSARY</u>
ONE ROOSTER
FOUR WHITE CANDLES
HONEY
WHITE WINE
MIXED DRY BEANS & RICE
RUM
CIGAR
PEMBA

1. Dig a large hole in the ground in the middle of a field.

2. Using pemba, draw the spirit signature of the Aje Spirits around the large hole and place the Mpaka of the Aje Spirits next to it. The hole will be directly in the center of the spirit signature.

3. Place the four white candles in all of the cardinal directions (north, south, east, west)

4. Light the candles.

5. Light the cigar and blow the smoke over the ritual area and directly into the hole.

6. Take a mouthful of rum and blow it over the ritual area and directly into the hole.

7. Invoke the Congo spirits using the traditional prayers.

8. If you do not know the prayers in Spanish/Congo then you can say it in English.

9. Cleanse yourself and the others who are present there with the rooster.

10. When you have finished, sacrifice the rooster and allow the blood to drip directly into the hole and directly on to the Mpaka of the Aje Spirits.

11. When the rooster is dead, place the body into the hole.

12. Pour honey over the body in the hole.

13. Wash your hands and the knife using fresh water and rum directly over the hole.

14. Pour red wine into the hole.

15. Using the four coconut shell chamalongo divination method, check to see if the offerings were accepted with blessings of the spirits.

16. If the spirits respond positive, cover the hole up with dirt and allow the candles to remain burning until completely finished.

It is also recommended that you light a sweet smelling or floral incense while doing the ritual.

A brass bell can also be used during the ritual. The Aje Spirits like the sound of ringing bells and all types of chimes. When they hear it they usually respond more favorabaly.

OCEAN RITUALS

A spiritual cleansing to bring peace and harmony. This cleansing can also be used in matters of infertility.

ITEMS NECESSARY
ONE GREY PIGEON
TWO WHITE CANDLES & TWO BLUE CANDLES
MOLASSAS
RED WINE
WHITE FLOWER PETALS
RUM
CIGAR
PEMBA

1. Dig a large hole in the sand near the water's edge.

2. Using pemba, draw the spirit signature of the Aje Spirits around the large hole and place the Mpaka of the Aje Spirits next to it. The hole will be directly in the center of the spirit signature.

3. Place the four candles in all of the cardinal directions (north, south, east, west)

4. Light the candles.

5. Light the cigar and blow the smoke over the ritual area and directly into the hole.

6. Take a mouthful of rum and blow it over the ritual area and directly into the hole.

7. Invoke the Congo spirits using the traditional prayers.

8. If you do not know the prayers in Spanish/Congo then you can say it in English.

9. Cleanse yourself and the others who are present there with the mixed dry beans & rice and afterwards drop it into the hole.

10. When you have finished, sacrifice the rooster and allow the blood to drip directly into the hole and directly on to the Mpaka of the Aje Spirits.

12. When the rooster is dead, place the body into the hole.

13. Pour honey over the body in the hole.

14. Wash your hands and the knife using fresh water and rum directly over the hole.

15. Pour white wine into the hole.

16. Using the four coconut shell chamalongo divination method, check to see if the offerings were accepted with blessings of the spirits.

17. If the spirits respond positive, cover the hole up with dirt and allow the candles to remain burning until completely finished.

It is also recommended that you light a sweet smelling or floral incense while doing the ritual.

A brass bell can also be used during the ritual. The Aje Spirits like the sound of ringing bells and all types of chimes. When they hear it they usually respond more favorabaly.

RITUAL TO INVOKE THE POWERS OF THE AJE SPIRITS

THIS SACRED RITUAL TO THE POWERFUL AJE SPIRITS IS USED TO REVERSE WITCHCRAFT AND NEGATIVITY.

STEP 1

1. Purchase a Red/Black Reversible Candle.

2. Anoint the Red/Black Reversible candle completely with Vic's Vapor Rub.

3. As you anoint the Red/Black Reversible Candle focus on your enemies and on the negative situation that you would like to see banished away from you.

4. Go out to a remote forest location which has many tall trees.

5. Draw the spirit signature of the *Aje Spirits* directly on the ground using pemba (White Chalk) in front of the base of a large tree.

6. Set the Red/Black Reversible Candle into the center of the spirit signature of the *Aje Spirits* and then light it.

7. Light sweet smelling incense.

8. Pour Bee's Honey over the spirit signature of the *Aje Spirits* and around the base of the Red/Black Reversible candle.

9. Pour Red Wine in and around the ritual area.

10. Using a metal bell, start to invoke the powerful *Aje Spirits.*

11. Using your right hand make the Catholic sign of the cross over your body and afterwards start ringing the metal bell while saying the following sacred invocation prayer:
(FACE THE NORTH DIRECTION WHILE RINGING THE BELL AND THEN TURN TO THE SOUTH, THEN TURN TO THE EAST AND THEN TURN TO THE WEST AND THEN TURN TO FACE THE RITUAL AREA WHERE THE CANDLE IS BURNING)

I CALL UPON THE GREAT FORCE OF THE UNIVERSE TO SURROUND MY BODY WITH PROTECTIVE LIGHT TO MAKE ME INVISIBLE TONIGHT SO THAT MY ENEMIES KNOWN AND UNKNOWN WILL NOT BE ABLE TO SEE NOR HEAR WHAT I AM ABOUT TO DO. I CALL UPON MY ANCESTORS WHO ARE KNEELING AT THE FOOT OF GOD IN LIGHT THAT THEY HEAR MY REQUEST AND GRANT ME SIGHT. OZAIN SEND ME A WIND, OZAIN SEND ME A BREEZE AND SUMMON THE SWEET SISTERS FROM THE NORTH, THE SOUTH, THE EAST AND THE WEST TO HEAR MY REQUEST AND TO PRESENT THEMSELVES HERE AT THIS TIME, THIS PLACE AND AT THIS CEREMONY TO WITNESS MY ACTIONS OF GOOD WILL SO THAT MY OFFFERINGS BRING GOOD AND LIGHT. I CALL UPON THE AJE SPIRITS, THE INVISIBLE MOTHERS OF THE NIGHT TO BE HERE BY MY SIDE. I CALL UPON THE AJE SPIRITS AND ASK THEM FOR THEIR DIVINE INTERCESSION. I HAVE NOT COME HERE TONIGHT TO FIGHT YOU OR TO CAUSE YOU HARM BECAUSE I KNOWN THAT I WILL NOT WIN AND SO THAT IS WHY I HAVE BROUGHT YOU THESE OFFERINGS AS A SIGN OF PEACE SO THAT YOU WILL HEAR MY REQUEST AND GRANT MY PRAYERS IN EXCHANGE FOR THESE SPIRITUAL OFFERINGS OF PEACE.

(SAY WHAT YOU WANT HERE)

I'AM HERE YOUR SON/DAUGHTER (SAY YOUR NAME). I HAVE BROUGHT YOU LIGHT, SO THAT YOU WILL LIGHT MY ROADS IN DARKNESS. I HAVE BROUGHT YOU THESE OFFERINGS SO THAT YOU WILL SWEETEN MY LIFE. I HAVE BROUGHT YOU INCENSE SO THAT MY PRAYERS WILL BE CARRIED TO WHERE YOU ARE. I ASK YOU THAT ALL OF THE GOOD THINGS IN MY LIFE. MY

MONEY, MY HEALTH, MY BUSINESS ETC... THAT WERE TAKEN UNJUSTLY AND STOLEN FROM ME BY MY ENEMIES THAT YOU BRING ALL OF THE GOOD THINGS BACK TO ME AND TO MY HANDS AT THIS VERY MOMENT FOR HERE WE STAND TOGETHER TO FIGHT A COMMON ENEMY. (SAY THIS 9 TIMES) FOR YOUR ENEMIES ARE MY ENEMIES AND MY ENEMIES ARE YOUR ENEMIES. (SAY THIS 9 TIMES) I CALL UPON THE SPIRIT EXU THE KEEPER OF THE CROSSROADS TO OPEN UP THE ROADS OF COMMUNICATION BETWEEN YOUR WORLD AND MY WORLD TO CONNECT THE DIVINE FORCE WHICH BINDS MAN TO THE GREAT COSMOS. I ASK YOU HERE AND NOW THAT WHAT EVER MY ENEMIES HAVE DONE IN THE PAST, ARE PRESENTLY DOING TO ME OR PLAN TO DO TO ME IN THE FUTURE THAT YOU PUNISH THEM 9X9X9 AND BRING THEM TO THEIR KNEES. WHATEVER THEY HAVE DONE OR PLAN TO DO TO ME REVERSE IT BACK TO THEM IN THE NAME OF DIVINE JUSTICE 9X9X9 SO THEY WILL RELIQUISH WHATEVER HOLD THEY HAVE OVER ME AND BE ON THEIR WAY. IN THE NAME OF THE GREAT UNIVERSAL FORCE I PRAY THIS TODAY. AJE BRILLUMBI NDOKI VIRA MUNDO (SAY 9 TIMES) WHO IS THE GREATEST IN HEAVEN – NZAMBI

<u>STEP 2</u>

Before leaving the ritual area, sprinkle sweet smelling spiritual pefume around the area and leave 9 pennies.

(YOU WILL KNOW WHEN THE AJE SPIRITS ARRIVE BECAUSE IT WILL START TO GET WINDY)

12. Before leaving the ritual area, place 9 pennies next to the burning candle.

STEP 3

13. After you have finished the *Aje Spirits* ritual return home and take a spiritual bath made from "Bay Leafs" for three consecutive days.

SPIRITUAL FOOD OFFERINGS TO THE AJE SPIRITS
(Ebo & Adimu)

Spiritual food offerings are one of the fastest ways to get a positive response for your spiritual requests from the Aje Spirits. When a spiritual offering consists of a blood offering or sacrifice (birds) or even an offering of cooked or raw meat, it is considered and referred to as an "*Ebo*". When a spiritual offering consists of flowers, perfume or wine, it is considered and referred to as an "*Adimu*".

Below you will find a list of some of the most common and acceptable Ebo spiritual offerings and Adimu spiritual offerings for the Aje Spirits.

Both types of spiritual offerings are used to appease the Aje Spirits and to also sweeten them to grant your spiritual requests. The type of spiritual offering offered to the Aje Spirits will depend upon what current spiritual situation you might be in. If you are in a very serious or life threatening situation, then the spiritual offering would usually be an "Ebo". If you are just asking for a general spiritual request then it more than likely will be an "Adimu".

EBO SPIRITUAL OFFERINGS

A plate of raw liver mixed with palm oil, honey and kosher rock salt.

A plate of cooked red meat covered in palm oil, honey and red peppers.

A plate of cooked pork with steamed vegetables.

A plate of cooked chicken covered in palm oil, honey and red peppers.

The blood from a rooster, hen or pigeon.

ADIMU SPIRITUAL OFFERINGS

A plate of cooked black beans and rice.

Flowers

Women's perfume

Red wine

Gin

Red peppers

Palm oil

Honey

Candles of all colors

Fresh fruit of any type

Fresh fruit juices

Sweet smelling incense

A plate of acorns

A plate of dried Indian corn

A plate of toasted corn with palm oil and honey.

Fresh herbs of any type.

Oak leafs

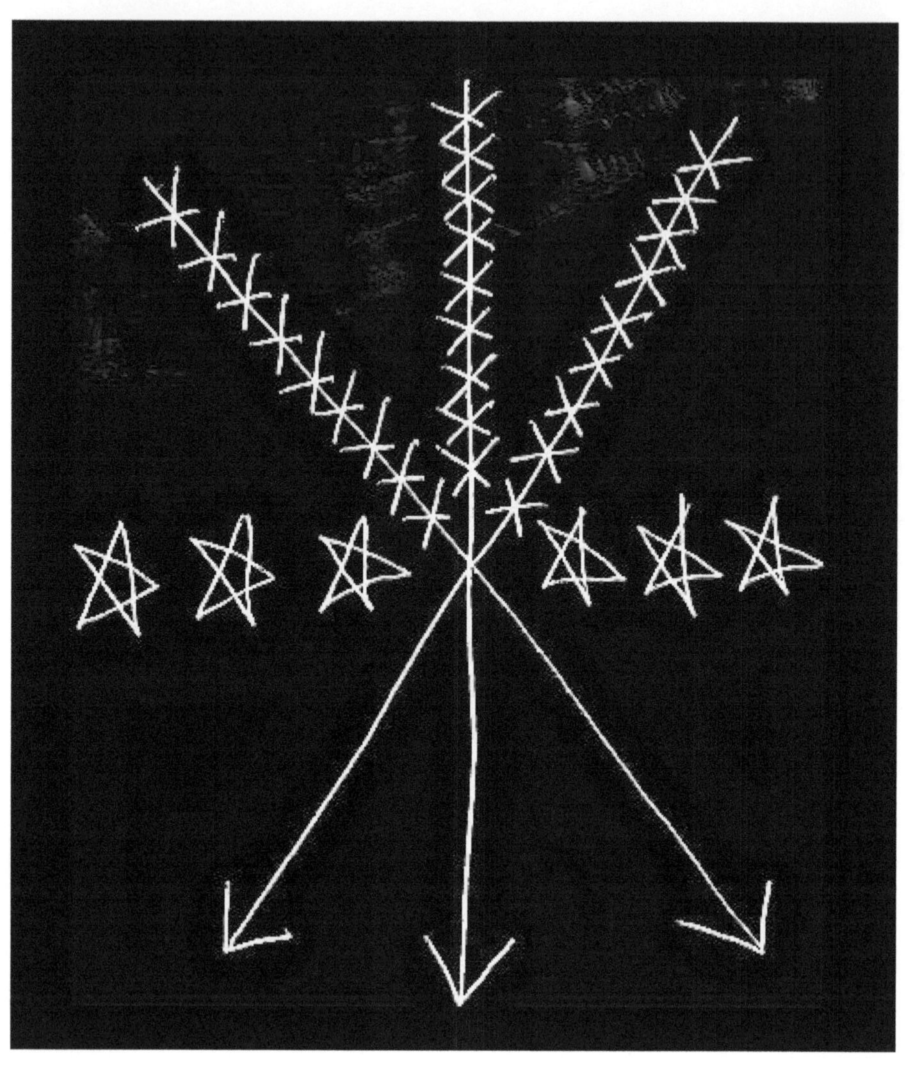

The Aje Spirit Signature that can be used in any of the rituals of this book.

SPIRITUAL OIL

www.ingramcontent.com/pod-product-compliance
Ingram Content Group UK Ltd.
Pitfield, Milton Keynes, MK11 3LW, UK
UKHW041924190726
13854UKWH00003B/1428